Vlad The Impaler

A Complete Introduction To The
Life And Work Of Vlad The Impaler

*(Most Crucial Rulers of Wallachia and His Impact
on the History of Romania)*

Reuben Hinman

Published By **Darby Connor**

Reuben Hinman

Vlad the Impaler: A Complete Introduction to the Life and Work of Vlad the Impaler (Most Crucial Rulers of Wallachia and His Impact on the History of Romania)

ISBN   978-1-998769-66-7

No part of this guidebook shall be reproduced in any form without permission in writing from the publisher except in the case of brief quotations embodied in critical articles or reviews.

Legal & Disclaimer

The information contained in this ebook is not designed to replace or take the place of any form of medicine or professional medical advice. The information in this ebook has been provided for educational & entertainment purposes only.

The information contained in this book has been compiled from sources deemed reliable, and it is accurate to the best of the Author's knowledge; however, the Author cannot guarantee its accuracy and validity and cannot be held liable for any errors or omissions. Changes are periodically made to this book. You must consult your doctor or get professional medical advice before using any of the suggested remedies, techniques, or information in this book.

Upon using the information contained in this book, you agree to hold harmless the Author from and against any damages, costs, and expenses, including any legal fees potentially resulting from the application of any of the information provided by this guide. This disclaimer applies to any damages or injury caused by the use and application, whether directly or indirectly, of any advice or information presented, whether for breach of contract, tort, negligence, personal injury, criminal intent, or under any other cause of action.

You agree to accept all risks of using the information presented inside this book. You need to consult a professional medical practitioner in order to ensure you are both able and healthy enough to participate in this program.

Table of contents

Chapter 1: Dracula's Connection.............. 1

Chapter 2: His Management 10

Chapter 3: His Credibility And Ruthlessness
.... 34

Chapter 4: Early Childhood And Birth..... 49

Chapter 5: Adolescence And Teenage
Years.. 54

Chapter 6: Highest Peak In Career Or Fame
.... 59

Chapter 7: The Person Behind The Fame 64

Chapter 8: Difficulties Of Life 68

Chapter 9: The Works 72

Chapter 10: What Lessons Can You Learn
From 80

Chapter 11: Interesting Facts 84

Chapter 12: Discussion Questions.......... 86

Chapter 13: Vlad The Impaler 92

Chapter 14: Portrait Of Vlad The Impaler From 1450 102

Chapter 1: Dracula's Connection

Vlad The Third, commonly referred as Vlad Dracula or Vlad the Impaler was Voivode of Wallachia 3x between the year 1448 to his death in 1476. He is considered to be one of the most significant rulers in Wallachian historical history and a national hero for Romania.

He was Vlad Dracul's 2nd child. He became the ruler over Wallachia in 1436. Vlad and Radu, their younger brother, were captured in the Ottoman Empire's Ottoman Empire in year 1442 to obtain their father's promise. Vlad's oldest brother Mircea and Vlad's father, John Hunyadi were killed when John Hunyadi was elected governor of Hungary. Hunyadi appointed Vlad's 2nd cousin Vladislav The Second as the new voivode. Hunyadi launched a military project against the Ottomans, with Vladislav accompanying him. Vlad went to Wallachia, with Ottoman support. Vladislav returned in October and Vladislav looked for refuge in Istanbul before the year ended. Vlad went to Moldavia or 1450 in the year 1449/1450, and later to Hungary.

Later, the relations between Hungary & Vladislav began to deteriorate. Vladislav invaded Wallachia in 1456 with Hungarian backing. Vladislav died fighting to overthrow him. Vlad ordered a purge in the Wallachian boyars, to strengthen his position. He was in dispute with Transylvanian Saxons. These supported Vlad's challengers Dan Laiota (2 of Vladislav's brother), and Vlad the Monk (his invalid half-brother). Vlad stole the Saxon villages and took the people he caught to Wallachia. He had them impaled, which motivated his cognomen. This was not a common occurrence. It had become a common pattern that would fear his enemies. In 1460 peace was restored.

Vlad was ordered by Mehmed the Second, Ottoman Sultan, to observe him. However, Vlad had Vlad's 2 envoys arrested and impaled. In February 1462, Vlad attacked Ottoman territories, killing 10s of countless Turks as well as Bulgars. Mehmed began a project to transform Vlad with Vlad's younger brother Radu. Vlad attempted to capture Targoviste's Sultan during the night 16--17 June 1462. The Wallachian Sultan and the primary Ottoman Army left Wallachia. However more Wallachians deserted Radu. Vlad went to Transylvania for help from Matthias Corvinus in the winter year 1462. Corvinus placed Vlad behind bars.

Vlad was held in Visegrad in captivity from 1463 to 1475. In Germany and Italy, stories about Vlad's ruthlessness spread during this period. Stephen the Third from

Moldavia requested that he be freed in the summer 1475. He was a soldier in Corvinus's army that fought the Ottomans in Bosnia at the start of 1476. Hungarian, Moldavian and Moldavian Soldiers helped him push Basarab Laiota out of Wallachia. He had dismissed Vlad's younger brother, Radu. Basarab returned before the year's end with Ottoman assistance. Vlad was killed in battle before January 10, 1477. Books that described Vlad's horrendous acts were some of the first bestsellers in German-speaking countries. A number of well-known Russian stories suggest that Vlad was able to consolidate the federal government's power only by using severe penalties. Numerous Romanian chroniclers also believed a similar view. Vlad's patronymic led to Bram Stoker's fictional vampire, Count Dracula.

Dracula was, until recently, referred to primarily as the name of an imaginary vampiric vampire. In diplomatic reports and stories, he was known as Dracula. His letters were signed by Draculya and Drakulya in the 1470s. His name is a slang term for his father Vlad Dracul (" Vlad the Dragon" middle ages Romanian), which he got after becoming a member of the Order of the Dragon. Dracula is Dracul's Slavonic Genitive Form. It refers to "the Dragon's child" or "the Dracula." Vlad's credibility was enhanced by modern-day Romanian dracul.

Vlad the Third is also known by the name Vlad Tepes, or Vlad the Impaler, in Romanian historiography. This refers to the impalement, his preferred method of execution. Tursun Be, the Ottoman author, called him Kazikli Voyvoda or "Impaler Lord" around 1500. Mircea the Shepherd (Voice of Wallachia) used this nickname when describing Vlad The Third in a letter on April the 1st, 1551.

Vlad's Youth and Beyond

Vlad the Second Dracul was the lawful second child. Mircea The First of Wallachia was an ineligible child. Vlad the Second earned the title "Dracul" due to his subscription in the Order of the Dragon. The Order of the Dragon is a militant brotherhood that was established by Holy Roman Emperor Sigismund. The Order of the Dragon was devoted to stopping the Ottoman expansion into Europe. Because he was still young enough to have a chance at the throne for Wallachia, in the year 1448. Vlad was most likely created in Transylvania, where his father had settled in the year of 1429. Radu Florescu, a Historian, claims Vlad was born in Sighisoara. It is believed Vlad was born there in Transylvania Saxon. Historiographers of the present day consider Vlad's mother to be either a child, a kinswoman or his father's unidentified first husband.

Vlad the 2nd Dracul invaded Wallachia after the death his half-brother Alexander II Aldea in 1436. One of his charters (which he provided January 20th 1437) contained the first reference to Vlad The Third and his older brother Mircea. This mentions them as their dads' "first born sons". Between the years 1437-1433, they were again mentioned in 4 files. Radu was the younger brother described in the final of 4 charters.

Vlad the 2nd Dracul disapproved of an Ottoman intrusion in Transylvania. This was after a meeting with John Hunyadi Voivode Transylvania. Murad the Second Ottoman Sultan had ordered him to Gallipoli in order to demonstrate his commitment. Vlad and Radu traveled with their father to Turkey, where they were all arrested. Vlad Dracul was eventually released, but Radu and Vlad stayed behind to secure their commitment. According to Ottoman narrates simultaneously, they were taken into custody in the fortress at Egrigoz (now Dogrugoz). Their lives were in danger because their father had supported Vladislaus, the King of Poland and Hungary during the Crusade at Varna 1444. Vlad the Second Vladacul was convinced his sons were "butchered in the interest of Christian peace". But neither Vlad nor Radu were killed after their dad's revolt.

Vlad Dracul recognized the sultan again and promised to pay annual tribute to him in the years 1446 or 14.47. John Hunyadi became the regent–governor in Hungary in the years 1446, and entered Wallachia the month of Nov 1447. Michael Critobulus, a Byzantine history expert, stated that Vlad and Radu fled to Turkey to escape their father's admiration. Vlad

Dracul's oldest child, Mircea was also killed. Hunyadi made Vladislav, the second child of Vlad Dracul, the ruler in Wallachia.

According to modern-day experts Vlad had two wives. Alexandru Simon (historiographer) suggests that his first spouse might have been the invalid daughter John Hunyadi. Jusztina Stilagyi, a cousin of Matthias Corvinus was Vlad's 2nd spouse. She was the widow Vencel Pongrac Szentmiklos's when "Ladislaus Drawlya" got married to her. It is most likely that it was in the year of 1475. She suffered Vlad Dracul. She first married Pal Suki, then Janos Earthelyi.

Vlad's oldest son, Mihnea, was conceived in the year 1462. Vlad's second unnamed child was killed prior to 1486. Vlad Drakwlya, Vlad's third child, failed to claim Wallachia in the year 1495. He was the founder of the Drakwla noble family.

Chapter 2: His Management

Let's find out what Vlad did on his many trips to conquer more terrain, and to bring more people under his control.

First Rule

Vlad was a possible complaintant in Wallachia following the deaths of his dad, and older brother. Vladislav The Second of Wallachia went with John Hunyadi to launch a project against Ottoman Imperial in September 1448. Vlad took advantage of his challenger's inexperience and burglarized Wallachia at an Ottoman army's head in October. He had to accept that the Ottomans had captured and reinforced the citadel in Giurgiu, on the Danube.

Hunyadi's Army was defeated in the Fight of Kosovo by the Ottomans between 17 and 18. October. Nicholas Vizaknai Hunyadi's deputy made it possible for Vlad to meet him at Transylvania. Vlad refused. Vladislav, the Second, returned to Wallachia to lead the remaining army. Vlad was forced by the Ottoman Empire to flee to Wallachia before December 7, 1448.

We are happy to share the news that Nicholas Vizaknai, a Nicholas Vizaknai correspondent, has asked us to be so kind regarding his request to meet him until John Hunyadi comes back from the war. We cannot do this because an emissary came from Nicopolis and told us with great certainty Murad had defeated Hunyadi. If we now come to Vizaknai, the Ottomans may come and kill us both. We ask you to be patient while we wait to see what Hunyadi is going through. If he does return from war, then we will be there to greet him and make peace. You will still be our enemies if you continue to fight the war, and you will be responsible for any consequences.

-- Vlad's Letter to the Councilors of Brasov

Vlad in Exile

Vlad was initially settled in Edirne (Ottoman Empire), shortly after his fall. Soon after his fall, Vlad moved to Moldavia. His father's brother-inlaw, Bogdan, and possibly his maternal uncle, had established the throne there with John Hunyadi. Bogdan, his child, was killed by Peter, the Third Aaron, in the October 1451 month. Stephen fled to Transylvania, where he sought support from Hunyadi. However, Hunyadi ended a three-year truce on November 20th with the Ottoman Imperial, acknowledging that the Wallachian boys had the right of choosing the inheritor to Vladislav, the Second, if they died.

Vlad probably wanted to settle at Brasov (which was the center for the Wallachian boyars expelled in Vladislaus' Second). But Hunyadi prohibited the Burghers from providing shelter to Vlad on February 6th 1452. Vlad returned to Moldavia from Moldavia where Alexandrel had dismissed Peter Aaron. His life events during the following years are not known. His return to Hungary must have been before July 3rd 1456. Hunyadi notified the Brasov people that he had charged Vlad the defense of Transylvania's borders.

2nd rule

These scenarios, as well as the date of Vlad's return to Wallachia, are not certain. Hungarian support was provided by Vlad to invade Wallachia in April July or August 1456. Vladislav, the Second, died just before the intrusion. Vlad sent the first letter he had as Voivode of Wallachia in his extant form to the burghers at Brasov on September 10. He promised that he would secure them in case the Ottomans invade Transylvania. But he also requested their support if they occupied Wallachia. In the exact same correspondence, he stated that "When a guy or prince is strong, he could make peace however he pleases, but when he's weak, another more powerful one will come to him and do what he wishes to him", which demonstrates his authoritarian personality.

Numerous sources (including Laonikos's chronicle), have noted that Vlad's orders at the start his reign saw hundreds, if not thousands of executions. He initiated a purge against boyars who were involved in the murders his father and senior brother. Chalkokondyles noted that Vlad "rapidly achieved a great change" and "entirely reinvented" the affairs of Wallachia by giving the "cash. property. and other products of his victims to his keepers. The list of members of Vlad's baronial Council during Vlad's rule shows that only 2 of them, Voico Dobrita (and Iova) managed to keep their positions from the years 1457 to 1461.

Dispute the Saxons

Vlad sent this popular homage to Vlad. John Hunyadi was killed on August 11th 1456. Ladislaus Hunyadi became his senior son and became the captain general of Hungary. Vlad was implicated by him of not being faithful to the king. The Sibiu burghers supported another pretender. "A priest of Romanians calls himself a Prince's kid." Vlad the Monk was Vlad's invalid brother. The latter seized Amlas that had been held by Wallachia rulers in Transylvania.

Ladislaus VI of Hungary executed Ladislaus Unyadi March 16th, 1457. Hunyadi's mom Erzsebet Szilagyi along with her brother

Michael Szilagyi encouraged disobedience toward the king. Vlad helped Stephen, the second child of Bogdan, to move to Moldavia. Vlad also stole Transylvania's towns and ransacked Sibiu. Vlad's story in German was that he brought men, women, and children from a Saxon community to Wallachia. He then had them impaled. Vlad's attack upon the Szilagyis boosted their position considering that the Transylvanian Saxons remained faithful to the king.

Vlad's agents joined the peace talks between Michael Szilagyi & the Saxons. According to their contract, the burghers and villagers of Brasov agreed that Dan would be expelled. Vlad promised that Sibiu's merchants would be able "purchase and/or trade" Wallachian products in exchange for Transylvania's Wallachian merchants. Vlad described Michael Szilagyi in a letter dated December the 1st in 1457 as "his Lord, and older brother".

Ladislaus Hunyadi, Matthias Corvinus' younger brother, was elected king over Hungary on January 24, 1458. He instructed the burghers at Sibiu to keep the peace. Vlad, who was three years old, declared himself "Lord of Wallachia and all the duchies Amlass and Fagaras". This demonstrated that he had taken both the Transylvanian traditional fiefs of the Wallachian rulers. Michael Szilagyi gave permission for the boyar Michael to settle in Transylvania (as an authority of Vladislav II of Wallachia and other Wallachian Boyars) in late March 1458. Vlad quickly had Michael executed.

Vlad asked the Brasov burghers to send artisans out to Wallachia in the month May. His relationship with the Saxons was strained before the end. According to academic theories, the dispute arose because Vlad prevented the Saxons entering Wallachia and made them sell their items at mandatory border fairs to Wallachian sellers. Vlad's protectionist tendencies, or border fairs, are not documented. Vlad, instead, stated that he always advocated open market in the year 1476.

The steel that a Wallachian Merchant had purchased in Brasov from the Saxons was taken by them without the merchant being able to pay back the cost. Vlad "raided & tortured" Saxon merchants as a reaction to the incident, according a Basarab Laiota's letter dated January 21st 1459. Basarab had settled down in Sighisoara. He claimed Wallachia. Matthias Corvinus backed Dan the third (who was in Brasov again) against Vlad. Dan the Third said that Vlad had Saxon merchants killed or burned alive in Wallachia.

You know that King Matthias has sent you and when I reached Tara Barsei with my message, the authorities, councilors, and old men from Tara Barsei sobbed at us about the important things Dracula did. How he didn't remain loyal to our Lord, king, and had made an agreement with the Ottomans. He captured all the merchants from Brasov and Tara Barsei that had entered peace to Wallachia. But he wasn't satisfied only with their wealth, he also imprisoned and impaled them all, 41 total. They were not enough. He became even more wicked when he gathered three hundred boys from Tara Barsei in Brasov and Wallachia. These boys he impaled, and some he also burned.

Basarab Laiota writes to Tara Barsei & Brasov councilors

Vlad beat Dan the Third and robbed Wallachia. Vlad attacked southern Transylvania. Vlad demanded that all

Wallachian refugees fleeing Brasov be expelled or punished during the events. Vlad dealt with the Brasov burghers, who were his "brothers in arms and good friends" on July 26th 1460. Vlad attacked the Amlas and Fagaras region on August 24th, to punish those regional occupants who had backed Dan the Third.

The Ottoman War

Konstantin Mihailovic served as a Janissary in Sultan's Army and noted that Vlad was unwilling to pay tribute to the sultan in an unknown year. Giovanni Maria degli Angiolelli, Renaissance historical analyst, wrote that Vlad hadn't been able to commemorate the Sultan for three years. While both records seem to suggest Vlad overlook the Ottoman Sultan Mehmed The Second's suzerainty, however, these works were written many decades later. Tursun Be, a secretary in Sultan's court, mentioned that Vlad only became hostile to the Ottoman empire when the sultan went on "long explorations in Trebizon" back in 1461. Tursun Beg says that Vlad started new settlements along with Matthias Corvinus. His spies promptly alerted the Sultan. Mehmed sent Thomas Katabolinos to Wallachia as his envoy. He ordered Vlad to reach Constantinople. He also sent secret directions for Hamza, the bey at Nicopolis, in order to catch Vlad, who had crossed the Danube. Vlad was able to discover the "deceit, hoax" of the sultan and captured Hamza & Katabolinos. They were then executed.

Vlad ordered the leader of the citadel, Giurgiu, to open the doors in proficient Turkish. He then executed the Ottoman authorities. He attacked and destroyed the Ottoman Empire along with the Danube. He wrote to Matthias Corvinus, letting him know about the army action. It was February 11, 1462. At the time of the project, he mentioned that more "23.884 Turks" and "23.884 Bulgarians" had been murdered at his command. Corvinus offered him his army support, declaring that he had broken off the peace with Corvinus "for the honor of the king" and the Holy Crown in Hungary, as well "for conserving Christendom and conditioning the Catholic faith." According to a Kaffa letter by the Genoese ruler, the relationship between Moldavia und Wallachia had become strife by 1462.

Vlad's intrusion had been discovered by Mehmed the Second. He raised an army of more 150,000 people, which was, according to Chalkokondyles "2nd in size only" to the one who occupied Constantinople the year 1453. According to certain historical analysts such as Nicolae Stoicescu and Radu Florescu (consisting Franz Babinger and Radu Florescu), the army size indicates that the

Sultan wanted to live in Wallachia. Mehmed had, however, granted Wallachia prior to the invasion, which shows that Mehmed did not intend to change the ruler in Wallachia.

The Ottoman fleet made its landing at Braila in May. Braila was the only Wallachian Port on the Danube. On June 4th 1462, the Ottoman principal army crossed the Danube with the command of Nicoplis the sultan. Vlad, outnumbered and outnumbered by his enemy, chose a scorched Earth policy and moved toward Targoviste. Vlad stole the Ottoman camp and tried to capture or kill him during the night between 16 June and 17 June. Vlad could have won the battle against the Ottoman Army by either being in jail or dying. However, the Wallachians "really missed" the court of his sultan and attacked the tents of Isaac and Mahmut Pasha. Vlad and his associates fled the

Ottoman Camp at dawn after they failed to attack the Sultan's camp. Mehmed reached Targoviste in the middle of June. Chalkokondyles reports that although the town had been abandoned, the Ottomans found a "forest" of the impaled (many stakes filled with the corpsses of executed prisoners) in Targoviste.

The area of the Impalements consisted of seventeen stades and was 7 stades across. There were huge stakes on which it was reported that about twenty thousand children, men, and women had been spitted. It was quite a sight for both Turks and the Sultan. The sultan was astonished and said it was impossible to deny his nation a man with such great deeds and a wicked understanding about how to govern his country and its people. He added that a man who has done such things is well worth it. The Turks were shocked at the sheer number of men who were on the stakes. Babies had become too attached to their mothers and birds had created nests in their entrails.

-- Laonikos chalkokondyles, The Histories

Tursun Be noted that the Ottomans suffered from heat and thirst in the summer. The sultan decided not to go back to Wallachia and marched towards Braila. Stephen the Third, a Moldavian, rushed to Chilia (now Kiliya), to take the important citadel where a Hungarian Fort had been placed. Vlad also left Chilia to fight the march of Vlad's army. However the Ottomans prevailed over the Wallachians and Vlad returned to Moldavia. Stephen of Moldavia suffered injuries during the siege in Chilia. Vlad returned to Moldavia to recover.

Vlad's brother Radu and his Ottoman troops remained in Wallachia. Radu sent messages to Wallachians to remind them that the Sultan could again attack their country. Radu was defeated in battle by Vlad and his Ottoman Allies. But, more Wallachians disowned him. Vlad fled to Carpathian Mountains in the hope that Matthias Corvinus might help him restore his throne. Albert of Istenmezo had in mid August advised that Radu would be recognized by the Saxons. Radu made a deal with the Brasov burghers for validation of their industrial advantage and payment of 15 thousand ducats.

Hungary: Get behind bars

Matthias Corvinus reached Transylvania in November 1462. While the negotiations between Corvinus (and Vlad) lasted several weeks Corvinus decided not to wage war with the Ottoman empire. John Jiskra (Czech mercenary leader) captured Vlad at Rucar in Wallachia on the order of the King.

Corvinus presented three letters, written by Vlad, on November 7th 1462, to Mehmed II, Mahmud Paha, and Stephen from Moldavia. They were allegedly written by Vlad to clarify Vlad's sentence to Pius the Second. According to the letters Vlad offered his support to the sultan in his army against Hungary if he reestablished his throne. Most historical analysts agree that Vlad's time in jail was imposed by the creation of these files. Antonio Bonfini who was Corvinus's court historian admitted that Vlad's sentence was not explained. Florescu writes that "The style of writing and the rhetoric of meek submission (hardly fitting with what is known about Dracula), awkward Latin and awkward phrasing are all signs that the letters cannot have been written on Vlad's command." Florescu links the writer of the fake with a

Brasov Saxon priest

Chalkokondyles reports that Vlad was originally placed in prison "in the City of Belgrade" which is now Alba Iulia in Romania. He was finally taken to Visegrad, and was held there for 14 more years. We have lost all files about Vlad between 1462-1475. Stephen the Third sent his envoys from Moldavia to Matthias Corvinus in the summer of 1475. He asked him to send Vlad to Wallachia against Basarab Laiota. Basarab Laiota had previously submitted himself to Ottomans. Stephen wanted Wallachia to be protected for a ruler who had been against the Ottoman Empire. This was simply because, according his letter, the Wallachians "resembled the Turks" in the Moldavians' eyes. Vlad was only released when he converted, according to Slavic tales.

Catholicism

Death and third rule

Matthias Corvinus recognized Vlad as the legal Prince of Wallachia. He didn't offer him support in arming his principality. Vlad settled down in Insect. Vlad was the one who executed the leader of the group of warriors that broke into Vlad's home in Insect to chase a burglar. The Slavic stories tell Vlad that they did not have his authorization to enter the home. Vlad transferred to Transylvania on June 1475. In order to settle in Sibiu, Vlad sent his envoy to that town in the early part of June. Basarab Laiota, the legal ruler of Wallachia, was acknowledged by Mehmed the Second. Corvinus ordered that the burghers and heirs of Sibiu give Vlad 200 golden florins. Vlad went to Buda instead.

Vlad bought a Pecs home that became Drakula haza (Dracula's "home" in Hungarian). John Pongrac of Dengeleg was Voivode Transylvania's January 1476. He advised the people to send Vlad all the advocates of Vlad who had settled in the area, as Corvinus Laiota (Voice of Transylvania) had already signed a treaty. The relationship between Basarab, Transylvanian Saxons, and Basarab remained tense. Basarab was eventually defeated by Basarab's rivals. Corvinus dispatched Vlad to battle the Ottomans in Bosnia, along with the Serbian Vuk Grugurevic. They captured Srebrenica and other citadeles within the month of Feb and March 1476.

Mehmed The Second attacked Moldavia. He defeated Stephen the Third during the Fight of Valea Alba, July 26th 1476. Vlad and Stephen Bathory entered Moldavia. According to Matthias Corvinus, the sultan was required to raise Targu Neamt, the fortress, in late august. Jakob Discontent, who was synchronized, added that Vuk grgurevic and a member honorable Jaksic also participated in the resisting the Ottomans in Moldavia.

Matthias Corvinus commanded the Transylvanian Saxons of Wallachia to support Bathory's prepared intrusion into Wallachia on Sept 6th 1476. They also received notice that Stephen from Moldavia would also attack Wallachia. Vlad remained in Brasov where he confirmed the Wallachia regional burghers' business advantages on October 7th 1476. Bathory and his forces captured Targoviste in the Ottoman Empire on eight November. Vlad and Stephen from Moldavia formally confirmed their alliance. Basarab Laiota was forced to flee to the Ottoman Empire for refuge on 16 November. Vlad notified Brasov's merchants about Vlad's victory, and advised them that they should come to Wallachia. He was crowned on or before 26/11.

Basarab Laiota was sent back to Wallachia by the Ottomans, and Vlad died fighting for them in late January 1476 or early 1477. Stephen the Third, a third-generation Moldavian, wrote that Vlad's Moldavian retinue had been killed in a January 10th 1477 note. Leonardo Botta is the Milanese ambassador. He claims that Vlad was killed by the Ottomans. Bonfini said Vlad's head went to Mehmed, the Second.

Unknown is the exact location of his burial. Vlad was believed to be buried in Snagov Abbey according to a well-known custom. However, DinuV.Rosetti discovered no burial spot below the presumed "unmarked gravestone" of Vlad within the abbey. Rosetti reported, "Under the tombstone credit to Vlad there wasn't a burial place. There were only many bones and the jaws of horses. Constantin Rezachevici, a historian said Vlad was probably buried in the Comana Abbey first church. It was built by Vlad and is close to the battleground where Vlad was killed.

Chapter 3: His Credibility And Ruthlessness

Vlad's cruel acts became popular throughout his entire life. They were promoted by Matthias Corvinus' courtiers after his arrest. Niccolo Modrussiense the papal delegate had already written an article about such stories to Pope Pius in the year 1402. The pope added them to his Commentaries two years later.

Michael Beheim, Meistersinger wrote a long poem on Vlad's deeds based on his conversations with a Catholic monk that had managed to escape Vlad's jail. Von ainem wutrich der heisTrakle waida von der Walachei ("The Story Of A Despot Called Dracula and Voievod from Wallachia") was performed in the Winter Season of 1463 at the court Frederick III, Holy Roman Emperor in Wiener Neustadt. Beheim claimed that Vlad had 2 monks impaled in order to help them reach paradise. Also, he ordered the impalement and execution of their donkey for braying following its masters' deaths. Beheim also accused Vlad in duplicity. He said that Vlad had promised support to Matthias Corvinus (the Second) but didn't keep the promise.

Gabriele Rangoni, Bishop in Eger, and a former papal representative, realized that Vlad had been jailed because of his ruthlessness. Rangoni also mentioned that Vlad caught rats while he was in prison. Antonio Bonfini also mentioned anecdotes of Vlad in Historia Pannonica from 1495. Bonfini wanted both to validate the elimination and repair of Vlad, as well as Matthias's actions. Vlad was described as "a guy with unheard ruthlessness & justice". Sebastian Munster, in Cosmography, repeated Bonfini's tales about Vlad. Munster also noted Vlad's "credibility for despotic Justice".

... Turkish messengers came by Vlad to pay aspect, but they refused to remove the turbans. Vlad reinforced their custom by nailing 3 spikes to their heads so they couldn't take their turbans off.

-- Antonio Bonfini: Historia Pannonica

German stories

In Low German, the Holy Roman Empire released works including stories about Vlad's ruthlessness before 1480. Although they mention Vlad's project over the Danube in early 20142, the stories don't actually describe Mehmed, the Second's intrusion into Wallachia in June that year. They contain a detailed story of the disputes between Vlad (Transylvanian Saxons) and demonstrate that they were written "in to the literary minds the Saxons".

Vlad's Ransacking Raids in Transylvania are clearly based on eyewitness accounts.

These include the exact details of the raids and the list of churches destroyed by Vlad. They refer to Vlad as a "lunatic, psychopath, a sadists, a brutal killer, a mason" even worse than Caligula. Despite this, Vlad's ruthlessness stories should be considered carefully as they were most likely exaggerated (and even developed!) by the Saxons.

The invention of movable-type printing was a major factor in the popularity of Vlad's stories, making them one the first "bestsellers" in Europe. The books were issued in woodcuts, which featured dreadful scenes. This was done to boost sales. Editions in Nuremberg (1499) and Strasbourg (1500) depict Vlad dining around a table surrounded on all sides by passing-away people or poles.

Vlad constructed a huge copper cauldron with holes and covered it in wood. He then put the people in the copper cauldron.

Then he devised horrifying, horrific, and unorthodox tortures. He also ordered that mothers be impaled along with their newborn children on the exact identical stake. The infants protected their lives at the bosoms of their mothers until their deaths. He then cut the breasts off the women and put the infants into the car headfirst.

Dracula, a nasty autocrat (No. 12-- 13).

Slavic stories

The Skazanie o Drakule voievode, the Tale about Voivode Dracula, has more than twenty articles. These articles were written between the 15th-18th century. The documents were written by Russians, but they copied an original text from South Slavic. They include expressions which are foreign to Russian, but that are still used in South Slavic idioms, such as diavol (for "wicked") Original text was written in Buda during the 1482-1486 years.

The Skazanie contains 19 stories that are more extensive than the German anecdotes of Vlad. Raymond T. McNally said that they were a mix between facts and fiction. According to Raymond T. McNally the stories are mixed of fact and fiction. Skazanie describes Vlad as a "depised taking so strongly...that anyone who triggered any wicked, break-in... didn't live long". This promoted public order and the German story about Vlad's project to destroy Ottoman territory highlighted his harsh actions, while Skazanie emphasised his diplomacy calling it "zlomudry", "evil-wise". Even so, Vlad was criticized by the Skazanie for his conversion into Catholicism. They also linked his death with this apostasy. Some aspects of the anecdotes were later included in Russian stories about Ivan of Russia.

You must be able to assert yourself in the face of modern-day challenges.

Vlad's mass killings would have been considered war crimes and genocide if he had not committed them indiscriminately. Ioan Mircea Pascu from Romania was the defense minister. He stated that Vlad would be tried for his crimes against humankind at Nuremberg.

National Hero

The Cantacuzino Chronicle was Romania's first historical work to record a story on Vlad the Impaler. It tells the tale of the impalement and trial of Targoviste's boyars for Dan's murder. The chronicle also stated that Vlad drove the young boyars along with their spouses to build Poenari Castel. Neofit I the Metropolitan of Ungro– Wallachia spoke out about the

Poenari Castle legend. Constantin Radulescu Codin, an instructor from Muscel County (where the castle was located), released a regional legend in the early twenty-century about Vlad's grant letter written on bunny skin for the villagers who had assisted him to escape Poenari Castle to Transylvania after the Ottoman invasion. Radu Negru, a famous Romanian author, is credited with the contribution in other cities.

Radulescu Codin also mentioned other legends about Vlad that were also found in Slavic and German versions of Vlad's stories. This suggests that Vlad's stories are still a part of oral tradition. In the Slavic and German anecdotes, there are tales about Vlad burning the poor, lazy, and the disabled, as well the story of the execution for the woman who made her husband too short a shirt. Vlad's sobriquet was a reference to the regular impalements that were occurring during his reign. But the peasants told the tales and said that such cruel acts could not guarantee public order in Wallachia.

Vlad was a Romanian ruler who many artists consider to be a good man. He also executed unpatriotic boysars in order to support the main federal government. Ion Budai -Deleanu composed the first Romanian legendary poem focusing on Vlad. Tiganiada of Deleanu (Gypsy Legendary), which was published only in 1875 (roughly a century after it was compiled) depicts Vlad as a hero fighting off the Ottomans, boyars and strigoi, and other fiends at one end of an army made up of gypsies or angels. Dimitrie Bolintineanu praised Vlad's successes in his Fights to the Romanians, which was published in the middle part of the nineteenth-century. Vlad was considered a reformer who used violence to end the deplorable rule of the boyars. Mihai Eminescu, one the greatest Romanian poets, wrote The Third Letter, an historical ballad dedicated to the Wallachian noble princes. Vlad is encouraged to go back to the tomb and exterminate his nemeses.

You must be here, O fear Impaler.

Divide them into 2 sections, here are the fools, and there are the rascals.

They should be forced into 2 additions in the middle or the night.

The cells in prison and lunatic asylum were then illuminated.

-- Mihai Eminescu, The 3rd Lett.

Theodor Aman was a painter who illustrated Vlad's meeting and Ottoman envoys. It demonstrated the fear of Wallachian rulers.

Romanian historical analysts consider Vlad to be one of the best Romanian rulers. This is despite his insistence on the sovereignty of Romanian lands. Vlad's acts were often described as acts of logic serving the national interest. Alexandru Dimitrie.Xenopol is just one of many historiographers who first highlighted the fact that Vlad could stop the internal battles among the boyar groups only through his acts of terror. Constantin C. Gianu said that Vlad's orders for torture and execution were not made out of pity, but because he had a good reason to do so, which was often an important reason for state. Ioan Bogdan was not the only Romanian chronicler to refuse this brave appearance. Vlad Tepes (and the German- and Russian Stories) was Bogdan's 1896 work. He stated that Vlad should be forgiven by the Romanians rather than being presented as "a design to bravery or patriotism". A viewpoint survey was conducted in 1999 and 4.1% of respondents chose Vlad the Imaler as one "the most fundamental historical characters that have influenced the fate for the Romanians positively".

Vampire Folklore

Vlad, a story about Vlad made him one of the most popular middle-ages rulers of the Romanian land lands in Europe. Bram Stoker's Dracula, published in 1897, was the first to connect Dracula and vampirism. Stoker was first attracted by Emily Gerard's 1885 post about Transylvanian Superstitious Thoughts to Dracula. William Wilkinson's book, Accounts of the Principalities and Moldavia: Political Observations Relating To Them, was released in 1820. He provided limited information on the Middle Ages history of Wallachia.

Elizabeth Miller stated that Stoker knew nothing about Vlad the Impaler. According to Miller, it was therefore "obviously not possible to conclude that Vlad was the motivation of" Count Dracula. Stoker claimed that Dracula was Szekely's beginning because he knew nothing about Attila Hun and the Hunnic origin of the Szekelys. Wilkinson, Stoker's primary source, agreed with the German stories' reliability and called Vlad an evil man. Stoker did not make any recommendations for the historical figure in his working papers. Instead, he called the person 'Count Wampyr,' which is what all of his drafts are. Stoker received the name and other information from Wallachia about Wallachia's history for his book about Count Dracula.

Appearance and representations

Niccolo Modrussa the legate of Pope Pius, the Second, painted the only known extant description Vlad, whom he had first met in Buda. Innsbruck's Ambras Castle houses a reproduction of Vlad's photo. Florescu stated that the photo depicts a "strongly-set, harsh, in some way tortured" man with "big and deep-set eyes, dark green and permeating vision". Modrussa claims Vlad was dark-haired but Florescu says the color is not clear. Vlad's lower lip is visible in the photo.

Certain Renaissance paintings reveal Vlad's bad reputation in German-speaking parts. He was seen amongst the martyrs of Saint Andrew in a 15th-century painting. This painting is in the Gazebo at Vienna. Vlad is only one of many witnesses to Christ's Calvary at Calvary, in a St. Stephen's Cathedral church in Vienna.

Vlad was not very tall, but he was extremely stocky, strong, and had a cold, awful appearance. His nose was inflamed, his nostrils were inflamed, and his face was thin and reddish. His eyes were large and open, and the long eyelashes made it look intimidating. His face and neck were shaven with a moustache. The inflamed temples enlarged the head. A bull's neck joined to his head. From there, black curly hairs held on to his wide-shouldered individual.

Chapter 4: Early Childhood And Birth

Vlad III, or Vlad the Impaler, was a transylvanian prince who was born in Sighisoara. (Modern-day Romania). While historians agree that Vlad III was born in Transylvania most of them believe otherwise. Others believe that Vlad III was born in Sighisoara (modern-day România) and this idea came from Vlad III's connection with Stoker's Dracula. Many people believe Vlad III wasn't born in Transylvania. However, others believe he was actually born in Wallachia. Live Science states that Dracula can be linked to Transylvania. But Vlad III, who is the true, historical Dracula never owned any property in Transylvania. Curta suggests that Vlad III, the father of Vlad II, owned a Sighisoara, Transylvania residence. However, it's not certain that Vlad III is born there. It is possible Vlad the Impaler could have been born in Targoviste. Targoviste was then the royal seat for the principality, Wallachia. His father, Vlad II, was a 'voivode' (or ruler).

The exact location of Vlad III's birthplace is open to debate. However, many other matters are settled, including Vlad III's lineage. He was the first child of Vlad II Dracul, Princess Cneajna (Moldavia) and Princess Cneajna (Moldavia). He was the third of four children. It's interesting that Vlad III's father was an illegitimate child from a Wallachian noble. He spent most his youth at the court Sigismund (Luxembourg), who was also the king in Hungary and would eventually become the Holy Roman Empire's future Emperor.

Vlad III, the father of Vlad II Dracul, was welcomed into the Order of the Dragon Christian Military Society in 1431. This society was founded in 1408 by Sigismund de Luxembourg. Historiographical reports say that the Order of the Dragon was "similar in structure to the medieval crusaders. It consisted of 24 high-ranking knights who pledged to resist heresy, and to end Ottoman expansion. Vlad II joined the Order of Dragon and was given the surname Dracul, which means Dragon.

Vlad III was just 5 years old when Vlad II Dracul became the sovereign or voivode of the Principality, Wallachia, by Sigismund, Luxembourg. Their family then moved to Targoviste's mountainous region. According to sources "[Wallachia] was located between Christian Europe & the Muslim lands the Ottoman Empire. Transylvania & Wallachia were frequently scene of bloody fights as Ottoman forces pushed westwards into Europe and Christian Crusaders repulsed them or marched toward the Holy Land."

Vlad III was born into Draculesti and his parents taught him how to be a "voivode". As such, he was provided with a top-notch education and thrived. Vlad III was a child and loved to see the condemned men being led from prison to the platform, where they would be hanging.

Vlad III's father Vlad II had sworn allegiance Sigismund or the Christian Crusade but he did not keep to that covenant and switched to the Sultan of the Ottoman Empire.

Vlad III was just eleven years old, when his father and younger brother Radu Fair went to the Ottoman court in 1442 for a meeting. Following their conversations with Vlad II Dracul Vlad III was arrested by Sultan Murad II and they were held prisoner for several months. James S. Kessler of Echoes of Empires argues Vlad II "sent Vlad Junior (and his brother Radu cel Frumos) as 'royal prisoners' to an Ottoman court." Vlad III and his younger brother were used by the Sultan to secure collateral.

Vlad III and Vlad III were held captive in a Turkish castle while they were in prison. According to Smithsonian: "Archeologists in Turkey claim that they have found the Turkish prison where Vlad III was first kept." Excavations of Tokat Castle, northern Turkey, revealed secret tunnels as well as two dungeons. Hurriyet Daily News in Turkey "reported" that the restoration work started in 2009. The latest project to restore the castle's defense bastions was finished in the last ten days. These tunnels and lanes were discovered by Ibrahim Cetin who was one of the archeologists involved in the discovery. Cetin reported that "the castle's entire perimeter is covered with secret tunnels." It is very mysterious. It is extremely mysterious." While they could not give any details about the evidence, they were certain that Vlad III was kept there with his brother.

Chapter 5: Adolescence And Teenage Years

While held in Turkey as royal prisoner, the boys were educated in philosophy, science, and the arts. Vlad III and his younger brother were not only educated in these areas but also taught how to be horsemen and soldiers. The good times and bad came with the boys being held hostage. Some historians believe Vlad III, and Radu III were both torture victims and were subject to the Sultan's whims. Their fate depended on their father's political actions. According to the Ottoman chronicles of the time, the boys' lives were at greatest risk after their father supported Vladislaus in Poland and Hungary's defeat of the Ottoman Empire during Crusade de Varna in 1444. However, Vlad II believed that the boys would be killed "for the sake of Christian Peace."

Murad II, his son Mehmed I and their six-year-old sons lived with them for nearly six years. Radu the Fair did a better job adapting to life at Ottoman courts than his older brother. In fact, he converted Islam and became friends Mehmed II. There are many theories that Radu Fair might have been a Stockholm syndrome victim. This is an open question.

Miller said that the boys were given "fairly good treatment by current standards." "Nevertheless, Vlad was annoyed by his captivity. However, his brother accepted it and went to the Turkish side. Vlad held enmity. It was likely one of his motivations for fighting the Turks.

Some historical reports claim Vlad III saw individuals being held on stakes for the first time while he lived at the Ottoman court. Later on in his life, he used this tool to great effect. Another historical source suggests that the boys were probably sodomized. This is a common practice against Ottoman prisoners, and it was thought to be a way to keep them out heaven. The sultan intended to literally raise them and have them follow him when they would rule Wallachia.

Modern psychologists have spent a lot time investigating how Vlad III's turbulent childhood and violent upbringing may have impacted his later years. Some claim that his repeated abuse as a child by the Ottomans led to a hatred of Muslims and a visceral hatred that he carried into his later years. The Smithsonian says that Vlad's later bloodlust and desire for the Ottomans may have been a result of that trauma. Some scholars believe that this experience could have led to his sadistic tendencies -- namely, the urge to impale-- later in the life.

Vlad the Impaler (16 years old) was killed in the marshes close to Balteni, Wallachia.

Local Wallachian nobles (known locally as boyars) overthrew him. Historical reports such as John Akeroyd's The Historical Dracula claim that Mircea II, Vlad III's elder brother, was also killed. He was "tortured," blinded, and buried dead.

Vlad III was freed from his position as a royal prisoner after the death and burial of his father. Live Science reports, "Not long after those harrowing events in 1448 Vlad began a campaign to regain the seat of his father from the new ruler Vladislav I." Vladislav II was a Wallachian noble. Janos Hunyadi was the Hungarian regent. He was also the man who ordered Vlad II's assassination.

Florin Curta from the University of Florida is a professor of medieval and early modern history. He claims that Vlad III's "first attempt to the throne relied upon the military support of Ottoman Governors of the Cities along the Danube

River in Northern Bulgaria." Vlad also took advantage that Vladislav had not been there to fight the Ottomans.

Vlad III did win his father's seat but his time in Wallachia as voivode was cut short. Curta states that Vlad III was deposed only after two months. Vladislav I returned with the aid of Hunyadi and took the throne from Wallachia.

Although the cause of Vlad III's desire for revenge is still unknown, one thing can be certain: Vlad III began a war to secure his sovereignty almost immediately after he was released from Ottoman captive. He didn't intend on giving in without fighting.

Chapter 6: Highest Peak In Career Or Fame

Curta claims that there is little known about Vlad III's location between 1448-1456. It is known that Vlad III changed sides in the Ottoman/Hungarian conflict. He renounced his ties to the Ottoman governors for the Danube towns and received military support by King Ladislaus V. Hungary. Vladislav II also sought help from Mehmed II, the Ottoman ruler.

Vlad III was only able to demonstrate his military and political abilities in 1453 after Constantinople was destroyed. Live Science reported that "the Ottomans were now in a position of invading all of Europe." This was bad news not for Hunyadi. But it was good news for Vlad III. He needed to march against Vladislav II once more in order to overthrow him again and take his rightful place as voivode. Vlad III used this distraction against his disadvantage in July 1456 as the Ottomans, Hunyadi, and their forces were fighting each other. Vlad III took with him a small army made up of exiled boys and Hungarian and Romanian mercenaries mercenaries. They led them against Vladislav III at Targoviste.

Elizabeth Miller, author A Dracula Handbook, wrote that Vlad III was made the voivode de Wallachia following his attack on Vladislav 2 at Targoviste 1456. Vlad III had already created his anti-Ottoman post. Miller claims that his first order of business was to cease paying an annual tribute the Ottoman sultan - a measure which had previously guaranteed peace between Wallachia (and the Ottomans)".

Vlad III now wanted to consolidate his power in a powerful position. To stop the ongoing conflicts between Wallachia's boyars, Vlad III had to first do one thing.

The threat of his father's overthrow would be eliminated if these conflicts were stopped. Constantin Rezachevici, author of Dracula. Essays on the History and Times of Vlad The Impaler claims that Vlad, during a banquet he gave at Targoviste's palace, ordered the impaling 500 Boyars (perhaps 50), with the accusation their'shameless inunity' was the root of Wallachia's frequent changing of princes.

Juan Jose Sanchez Arreseigor reported that Vlad III's reign began with a crackdown against crime. He used a zero-tolerance policy even for minor offenses, such a lying, according to a National Geographic article. He made commoners and foreigners his public servants, in an effort to cement his power. As voivode, his power was unlimited. He could appoint or dismiss and even execute his new employees at will.

This was just the beginning of many brutal events that led Vlad the Impaler to his posthumous name. The shameful disunity of the victim and the subsequent punishment are well documented. Miller states, "In the 1460s or 1470s, right after the invention of printing presses, a lot these stories about Vlad were circulated orally. After that, they were assembled by different individuals in pamphlets, printed."

There is no way to know if the Vlad III horror stories were completely true or if embellishments were made along the route. Miller said that several pamphlets from this period tell nearly the same horror stories about Vlad. She believes these tales are at most partially historically accurate. It is not clear, however, just how fierce Vlad III was. Dracula Sense and Nonsense has a quote from a monk, who said Vlad III was a "fierce, yet just ruler" in her book.

Vlad III's brutal displays continued, whether they were embellished. Kristen Wright (Disgust and Desire:The Paradox of the Monster) claims that Vlad III was responsible of impaling dozens of Saxon traders who had previously allied themselves with the boys. According to historical records, it was not dozens, but many Saxon merchants. A group of Ottoman ambassadors refused to remove their turbans, possibly due to religious reasons, while having an encounter with Vlad III in 1456. McNally and Florescu say that he replied by promising them that the turbans would "forever remain on their heads" and having the head coverings nailed onto their skulls.

Chapter 7: The Person Behind The Fame

Vlad III was married twice. Vlad III had a son and a daughter with his first wife, but little is known. His name is Mihnea the Evil. He was the prince of Wallachia. Vlad III's first marriage is believed have ended in 1462. Vlad III was fighting the Turkish at that time. Legend has it that Vlad III's castle at Poenari Castle had been completely surrounded by the Turkish army by the end the night. Radu the Fair led the Turkish army. Vlad III was his younger brother. Vlad III and his wife Vlad III decided to escape from the castle's highest tower and plunge into the Arges River below. Legend says she said that she would rather have her body eaten by the Arges fish than captured by the Turks. Vlad III was captured by King Matthias Corvinus (Hungarian ruler) and placed in prison after the death of his wife.

According to The History of Royal Women a article states that Vlad had to marry again after his first wife died. But, he continued to take mistresses throughout his captivity. One of his mistresses proved to be very unlucky. Vlad broke her body to prove she was pregnant.

Vlad III got married again after the death his first wife. Ilona Zzilagyi, his second wife was born. According to historical accounts, she was a fraternal niece of King Matthias Corvinus, Hungary's ruler. The number of children the couple had is unknown. Some historians believe they only had two children. Others argue they had a second child, whom they called Maria. Grunge says that Ilona is the daughter of a Romanian Noblewoman. Vlad, who was temporarily in prison by King Corvinus during his years in captivity, met her while she was there. When she married Vlad, she became his stepmother by marrying his first wife. This young man was named Mihnea. However, he chose to go by the equally descriptive nom-de guerre of Mihneathe Evil.

History tells us that Ilona was not in love with Vlad 3 although historians may claim so. Ilona was made to marry Vlad III as a condition of his freedom. Ilona was the chosen noblewoman. Reports claim that Ilona was the chosen noblewoman.

Vlad III and Ilona got married. After that, they moved to Buda, where Ilona and Vlad stayed in a grand palace. They had two sons. The first was Vlad IV. However, the second son is still unknown. Vlad III continued to fight and, in November 1475 he fought Basarab Lariota for the title de prince of Wallachia. Ilona, the Princess of Wallachia, won.

The History of Royal Woman reveals that Ilona, the princess of Wallachia, did not live long. Vlad III was killed in battle 1476. His stepson, however, suffered from low approval ratings. He was eventually assassinated in 1505. Ilona may have fled to Pest from her home to continue her years. Vlad, her oldest child, returned to Hungary to continue his service in the household Corvinus.

Chapter 8: Difficulties Of Life

Vlad III executed the Ottoman prisoners and sent them to prison in August 1462. After that Vlad III fled to Hungary. Vlad III was unable defeat Mehmed II, despite his military prowess. Vlad III was arrested during this exile. He was also married for a second time, and had two additional children.

Vlad III was exiled while Radu the Fair (his younger brother) took control of Wallachia. John M. Shea, the author Vlad the Impaler. The Bloodthirsty Medieval Prince. argues that Vlad was favoured to return to power after Radu died in 1475.

Radu the Fair passed away in 1476. After that, Prince Basarab was the Elder, a Turkish Danesti clan member. Vlad III made one more bold attempt to win back his post as the Voivode de Wallachia. He was supported by Stephen the Great, his cousin voivode, and Moldavia's voivode.

Prince Basarab and his army ran away from the castle after they arrived. While Vlad III was successful with his attempts, the throne did not last very long. According to historical records, Vlad III was removed from the ruler's seat by Stephen III with his forces. This resulted in Vlad III being left in a fragile and precarious situation. Reports indicate that Vlad III was unable to obtain support in time for Prince Basarab to return to the throne. Vlad's many cruelties over the years convinced the boyars that they would have a better chance under Prince Basarab. Vlad's cruelties made it difficult for the peasants to abandon him. Vlad had to confront the Turks, even though he had a small force of four thousand men at his disposal.

Like many other facts concerning Vlad III's story, there are many different versions of what Vlad III did to end his life. Many historians believe Vlad III was murdered in

1476, while fighting the Turks close to Bucharest. Some historians believe that he was killed during the same war against Turks by traitorous and disloyal Wallachian Boyars. Another historian suggests that Vlad III could have been "surrounded by the bodies his loyal Moldavian Bodyguards" during the war. Others suggest that Vlad III was actually killed accidentally by one of his own men. Although there are multiple theories on how Vlad III died of his injuries, most historians agree that Vlad III died in December 1476 at age 45. Philippa Gregory is a historical fiction author who recently published a novel called Vlad III. She documents in it that Stephen III of Moldavia had sent a "1477" letter to confirm Vlad the Impaler's death. They were attacked by the Ottoman Empire and Vlad was reportedly murdered. His head was sent to Sultan Mehmed II at Constantinople as an award.

Gregory's finding is confirmed by other sources. He claims that Vlad III's body had been decapitated and that his head was sent to Istanbul with honey preserves. The sultan placed it on a stake to show that Kazikli Bety (Vlad III), was indeed dead.

Chapter 9: The Works

Whitman: The Transcendentalist

Vlad III had a worthy rival in Mehmed II. They met several times on the battlefields. He conquered Constantinople by 1453 and less then a decade later, Mehmed II marched to Wallachia in 1462 with more than 90,000. According to historical records Vlad III used guerilla warfare in addition to night raids. He then "used his trademark tactic of impaling more that 23,000 prisoners with their families outside the city of Targoviste and putting them on show along the enemy's route." Matei Cazacu, the Romanian historian, says that Mehmed II saw the "forest of the dead" and turned around to march back to Constantinople.

Vlad III is reported by Mehmed I to have written Mehmed II after the display. He said, "I killed peasants," and that he also killed men and women living at Oblucitza (where the Danube flows into to the sea). We killed 23,884 Turks.

Another battle took place in June 1462. It would be known later as the Night Attack of Targoviste. Florescu claims that Vlad III's and Mehmed III's armies fought through a night "atthe foothillsof the Carpathian mountains." Florescu says that about 5,000 Vlad III's soldiers died, as opposed to 15,000 Ottomans. These men claim that it was an act "of extraordinary temerity," which is celebrated both in Romanian literatures and folklore.

Mehmed II and his force eventually left Wallachia. Vlad III however lost so many Wallachians in his brother Radu, the Fair, that in the end, he went into exile. He was then imprisoned at later 1462.

Despite 1462 being defeated in the end and Vlad III's acclaims still remained widely discussed. Vlad III's victory over his enemy caused word to spread quickly and was celebrated all across Wallachia, Transylvania and Europe. Curta states that Vlad III's positive reputation in Romania comes from the fact that he was considered a good character despite being a harsh ruler.

Vlad the Impaler's Legacy of Cruelty

Vlad III's cruelty was widely reported during his lifetime. These stories quickly became his legacy.

Michael Beheim had written a poem about Vlad III's cruelty. "Von ainem wutrich der heisTrakle waida Von der Wallachei," or the "Story Of A Despot Called Dracula", was the title of the poem. According to Michael Beheim, the poem was based upon the experiences of a Catholic Monk who was imprisoned by Vlad III. He managed to escape and continue to tell the tale. McNally states that Beheim said in one of Beheim's verses: "Vlad had 2 monks impaled for them to go into heaven. Also, he ordained the impalement to their donkey as it began to bray after its masters' deaths."

Vlad III's stories quickly became bestsellers in Europe by 13th century. One such publication published the stories with the title, "About a mischievous ruler called Draculavoda (No. 12-13). Vlad III, as described in the story, had "...built an enormous copper cauldron. He then placed a lid made from wood with holes on top. He put people in the cauldron, put their heads into the holes, and secured them. Finally, he filled the cauldron with water. The fire was lit under the lid. He invented horrifying, horrific, and new tortures. He ordered that all women were impaled with their newborn babies on the same stake. The babies fought to the death at their mother's breasts. He cut the breasts of his wife and placed the babies in the infants' heads.

Vlad III's actions in today's terms would undoubtedly be regarded as genocide. According to historical records, Vlad would have been convicted of crimes against humanity if he had been brought to trial at Nuremberg.

National Hero

Nicolae Balota is a Romanian academic who believes that The Cantacuzino Chronicle, "was the first Romanian historic work to record Vlad the Impaler's tale, and narrates his imprisonment by Targoviste's boyars for the murder in Dan."

Through history, many Romanian poets and artists have called Vlad III their national hero. Dimitrie Bolintineanu wrote the following poem, in which he celebrated Vlad III's victory during the Battle of Romania. He strongly believed

Vlad III had been a reformer. His brutality was "necessary in order to prevent the despotism a boyars." Mihai Eminescu, who is considered one of Romania's greatest poets wrote "The Third Letter" which is an excerpt of his feelings about Vlad III's rule.

You must make them understand, O dread Imaler.

They can be divided into two separate parts: here are the fools, and there are the rascals.

You can place them in two encloseds.

Then, light the fire in the prison and lunatic asylum.

-- Mihai Eminescu, The Third Letter

Vlad III is a name that many Romanian historians have used to describe him as "one the greatest Romanian rulers", emphasizing the fact that he fought for the independence of the Romanian land. Even though Vlad III was a strong advocate of national independence, others, such as Alexandru Dimitrie. Xenopol, feel that Vlad III would have struggled to end the internal conflicts within the boyars if Vlad III had not used terror. Constantin C. Gurescu, another historian, stated that Vlad III's order to execute and torture his subjects "were not motivated by caprice" and that they were carried out for a reason. This was, in part, the reason that Vlad III used, and that it was often the state. Ioan Bogdan, one among the few Romanian historians who don't believe Vlad III deserves his heroic appearance, is one such historian. Bogdan published Vlad Tepes along with the German Narratives and Russian Narratives back in 1896. In this work, Bogdan argued that Romanians ought to be ashamed about Vlad rather than presenting him in a role model of courage and patriotism.

A poll was carried out in 1999 to gauge the public opinion regarding Vlad III. Only 4.1% felt Vlad the Impaler was one "the most important historical figures who have influenced Romania's destiny for the worse," according to the results.

Chapter 10: What Lessons Can You Learn From

"Whatever's done for love will always be more than good or evil."

-- Friedrich Nietzsche

It is hard to doubt Vlad III's brutality. Even though historical records are exaggerated and embellished to some extent, they still prove Vlad the Impaler's name. However, it is worth asking why Vlad the Impaler did what he done. It might have been the love he had Wallachia. Or perhaps the love he held for his father or brother who were betrayed and murdered by their countrymen. Perhaps Nietzshe was right in that whatever is done out love is neither good, nor evil.

We won't be able to determine the motives of Vlad III, but most people will say that even though they were done for love, they were not sufficient reasons for him to resort violence.

Evil is defined by anything that causes "ruin or injury" or pain. It is also described as something that is harmful, destructive, and brings about misfortune for others. Now that we understand what evil is, maybe then we can ask, "Are people truly born evil?" Quora asks this question.

One person wrote that "I don't believe in evil people." Vlad III could be attributed for his evil nature if he is a product of his environment, upbringing and circumstances. Or was it a result his circumstances?

Another person stated that "the best thing I have learned is that pure evil persons really do exist." They are deeply flawed human beings. It's really difficult to change people with such a flawed mindset. They believe what their beliefs are." Perhaps this is true. Vlad III was evil in the sense that nothing could ever change him.

It is possible to learn from bad people if they do exist. Ryan Holiday wrote a Thought Catalog article entitled "Great Lesons from Bad People - Learning From History's Most Hated People" Ryan Holiday was inspired by Julius Caesar's belief that "fortune favors bold people" Genghis Khan's belief that "fortune favors them"; Fidel Castro's ability to "persuade, rather than command" and Jefferson Davis's warning about micromanaging.

Holiday says that every one of these "bad" people has something to learn from us. Holiday says that although we may think it is enough just to learn from those that we admire, anyone can learn. This only leaves half the lessons. The other half of the equation--and possibly the most important--requires us to learn from even those we find disgusting or appalling.

Plutarch said that fire is a deadly weapon, but it can also provide light and heat to those who are skilled at using it.

Vlad III may have been a villain, but perhaps there's something we can learn from him.

Chapter 11: Interesting Facts

Did you know?

Vlad III was born in Transylvania. This idea was sparked by his connection to Stoker's Dracula. Vlad III was actually born at Wallachia, one of Transylvania's most hated areas.

Did you know?

Vlad III was one the noble Sighisoara children when he was growing up. These children were special because they were prepared to take on future responsibilities while still being children. Sighisoara's noble children were taught how to trap Hares and spent the summer shooting eagles with slingshots.

Did you know?

Vlad III and his younger brother were detained by the Sultan. This made their lives much more difficult. However, they would improve their fluency over the six years that followed.

Did you know?

Vlad III was the master of psychology warfare. He used fear to conquer his enemies. Fear could be called Vlad III's greatest tool.

Did you know?

Vlad III, a controversial figure, is still being discussed today. Some historians say he acted only as others would during those times. Others disagree and argue that Vlad III was an unquestionable villain.

Chapter 12: Discussion Questions

Vlad III Dracula still stands out as one of the most important Wallachian leaders. He was infamous for his brutality, but he remains controversial because he is still viewed as both a hero (some people love him) and a villain (some don't). Can someone be both an antagonist and a hero at the same time? Discuss.

Discussion Questions

Vlad III, during his reign was responsible in the deaths of over 80000 people. His preferred method for killing his enemies was to impale them. Vlad III was also said to have drank the blood of his enemies. This belief inspired Stoker's creation of the terrifying and mysterious Vlad III. Why do you think Vlad III may have drank the blood of his enemies What purpose would it serve, you ask? Discuss.

Discussion Questions

Vlad III, the father of Vlad II Dracul, was welcomed into the Order of the Dragon Christian Military Society in 1431. This society was founded in 1408 by Sigismund (Luxembourg). Historical records state that the Order of the Dragon was modeled on the medieval crusaders. It was founded by Sigismund of Luxembourg. Why did he do this? Discuss.

Discussion Questions

Psychologists of today have spent a lot of time trying to understand how Vlad III's violent childhood, turmoulotus, and early years may have influenced him later on in his life. Some claim that his repeated abuse as a child by the Ottomans led to a visceral hatred of Muslims, which he carried into adulthood. The Smithsonian reports that some scholars attribute Vlad's later bloodlust to the Ottomans to that traumatic experience. They speculate that it may have led him to his sadistic tendencies (namely, impaling—later in the life). Are you unsure if Vlad III was born evil or if his life experiences made him that way?

Discussion Questions

Vlad III now wanted to consolidate power in a powerful position. To stop the ongoing conflicts between Wallachia's boyars, Vlad III had to first do one thing. The threat of his father's overthrow would be eliminated if these conflicts were stopped. Constantin Rezachevici, author of Dracula.

Essays On the Life And Times of Vlad The Impaler claims that Vlad, the Impaler, ordered the impaling, perhaps 500, of Boyars (or maybe only 50), in a banquet at Targoviste. He claimed that their "shameless inunity" was the reason for frequent changings of the princes of Wallachia. Discuss the actions of Vlad III. Also, discuss why Vlad chose to rule in fear from the beginning.

Discussion Questions

Miller claims that Vlad stories circulated orally between the 1460s & 1470s. After the invention the printing press was invented, many were collected in pamphlets by different people and printed. Discuss the effects of the printing press on information dissemination. How did this help or hurt people like Vlad III III?

Discussion Questions

There is no way to know if these terrifying stories about Vlad III were real or if they were embellished. Miller said that several pamphlets from this period tell nearly the same horror stories about Vlad. She believes these tales are at most partially historically accurate. But, it's debatable just how powerful Vlad III was. Dracula Sense and Nonsense has a quote from a monk, who claimed Vlad III was "fierce and just ruler". Discuss.

Discussion Questions

Holiday claims that every one of these "bad" people has something to share with us. Holiday says this is why "we believe it is sufficient to learn just from the people we admire--but anybody can do that. It only leaves half of what we can learn. The other half, and possibly the most important part of the equation requires us to learn from even people we hate or find appalling. Plutarch said that fire is a deadly weapon, yet it can provide light and heat to those who use it. Discuss what you think Vlad The Impaler has to teach us.

Chapter 13: Vlad The Impaler

We have broken the peace with the Ottomans, not for any benefit of ours, but for the honor of your Highness, and the Holy Crown of your Majesty, and for the preservation of the whole of Christendom, and for the strengthening of Catholic law. --- Vlad the Impaler

Portrait of Vlad Dracul, from 1433, the father of Vlad the Impaler

Literature from the 19th century contained several works in the science fiction genre that became extremely popular, and spread to all corners of the world. In these years, mystical and legendary themes came to the forefront, and these myths began to be used frequently in literary works. The main subjects of the stories contained wicked witches, scary ghosts, and gruesome creatures. However, vampire legends in literature were certainly the most sought after by the readers, since blood sucking immortals were unfathomable, and truly frightening.

Consequently, the following question will need to be asked to readers; have you read the novel by *Bram Stoker* titled, *Dracula*? The answer is surely yes, however, if there are a few people that has not yet, a brief summary is warranted. A reminder might be even necessary to those who have read it years prior.

Dracula is a gothic novel, which was published in the year 1897. The novel comprises of journal entries, letters, and telegrams written by the main characters. It begins with a young English lawyer, as he travels from *England*, to the faraway region in eastern Europe of *Transylvania*. The young lawyer plans to meet with *Count Dracula*, a client of his firm, in order to finalize the purchase of multiple property transactions in *London*, England. When he arrives in Transylvania, the locals react with terror and shock, after the lawyer discloses his destination as the Castle of Count Dracula.

This is how the novel begins, and grips the reader to continue on the interesting and exciting journey.

In complete reality, the legendary novel is about an old noble count, a vampire, from the eastern edge of the European continent. At the faraway mysterious land, Count Dracula constructs a plan to travel, and start a new life in England, where there are millions of victims for his choosing. The innocent and blind victims are not aware to the wise vampire counts mischievous plot to drink their blood, and to feed upon all of them in the still of the dark night.

There are only a few persons in the world that strike more fear into hearts than *Count Dracula*. The mysterious count has inspired countless horror films, television shows, and other shocking stories.

It has been speculated for the past century, but concluded now, the old noble count from the novel, was based on the historical figure of *Vlad the Impaler*. Nevertheless, Bram Stoker's Dracula was associated with Transylvania, but the real and historical Vlad the Impaler was not from this region of Europe. Vlad was from the close-proximate region of *Wallachia*, a vast mountainous area of eastern Europe, owned by the *Ottoman Empire.*

Why was Count Dracula inspired by the historical figure of Vlad? The reason was that Vlad impaled people regularly, and he became famous for various other cruel tortures committed. The blood, flesh, and corpses of the victims impaled were used to frighten his enemies. These strange and abnormal tactics used, created rumors about Vlad being a vampire; who drank the blood of his victims.

In 1431, *King Sigismund* of the Hungarian Empire, who later become the *Holy Roman Emperor*, recruited Vlad's father into a secret knightly order called, *Order of the Dragon*.

The father, Vlad Dracul was invited to the city of *Nuremberg*, here, he joined the secret dragon order, founded by knights, princes, and even kings, who were associated with various royal families in Europe. The order had 24 members, and all of them came from noble families; for this reason, the order became extremely powerful in Europe. The members of the order were given a necklace in the form of a dragon, which was made of precious stones. The members wore the striking necklace for the rest of their lives, and it was passed-down from a father to son.

The *Order of the Dragon* was dedicated to one mission, that being to defeat the *Ottoman Empire*, and to stop the empire's further advancement into Europe. Vlad Dracul's principality of Wallachia was situated between Christian Europe and the Muslim lands of the Ottoman Empire. It was often the scene of bloody battles where Christian armies drove the Ottoman janissaries eastward, but soon enough, the Muslim janissaries came back to reclaim their domain.

Vlad the Impaler was born in Wallachia in the year 1428, and was known popularly as *Vlad Dracula*, meaning, *Vlad, son of the dragon*. As a result of his father's participation in the order, the surname, *Dracul* was given to him. The surname, Dracul, meant, *dragon*, hence, Vlad's surname, Dracula, son of the dragon.

Vlad hated the Ottoman Empire as he was given over to the empire at a young age, by his father, *Vlad Dracul*. Underneath Vlad's dislike for the empire was not only being a prisoner in the empire, but the treatment shown to his father by the empire.

Vlad Dracul was the prince of Wallachia, but captured and imprisoned by the Ottoman Empire, in the city of *Gallipoli,* in the year of 1441 for over one year. Vlad Dracul had sided with the *Hungarian Empire*, during a war campaign against the Ottomans, nonetheless captured and sent to prison.

Vlad Dracul was released from prison, but first, he was required to pledge alliance to the Ottomans, and never support the enemies of the empire again. Also, Vlad Dracul was mandated to pay an annual tribute, plus send 500 boys from Wallachia each year to serve in the janissaries of the Ottoman army. Furthermore, the heaviest of the demands made by the Ottomans, Vlad Dracul was forced to give his two sons, Vlad the Impaler and *Radu the Fair*, as hostages to secure his complete loyalty in the future.

The future ruler of Wallachia, Vlad had multiple names, a few of them are as follows:

Vlad III,

Vlad Dracula,

Voivode the Impaler, and

Vlad Tepes.

In this book, he will be referred to as Vlad the Impaler.

Little is known about Vlad, *son of the dragon*, and his extremely close connection with the *Ottoman Empire*. In this book, Vlad's life will be examined, his relationship with the mighty empire, and the empires ruler, *Fatih Sultan Mehmet II*, the conqueror of *Constantinople* or *Istanbul*. The name Fatih translates as Conqueror.

Conqueror Sultan Mehmet II

Chapter 14: Portrait Of Vlad The Impaler From 1450

Portrait of Vlad the Impaler from 1450

Vlad and Radu the Fair were the sons of Vlad Dracul. To secure the support of the Ottoman Empire, and to show goodwill and complete loyalty, he was forced to give his two young sons to the empire. Therefore, the Ottomans allowed Vlad Dracul to remain at the head of the kingdom in Wallachia, in-return for paying yearly tribunes, and as stated previously, his two sons were taken as hostage.

In the Ottoman Empire, a new beginning starts for the brothers, meaning the *Devshirme* period begins for both. The empires Devshirme Policy was to educate foreigners, mostly young boys in the different educational institutions. It was to make them loyal, establish emotional bonds, and build trust with them and the mighty empire.

Vlad and Radu were taken in 1442, and sent first to *Kutahya*, a city in western *Anatolia*. After living here for a few months, the brothers were sent to the distant city of *Tokat*, located in northern Anatolia, to live in the castle of this city. The brothers lived here for less than one year, and finally they were sent to the capital city of *Edirne* or *Adrianople* of the Ottoman Empire.

Evliya Celebi, who was a writer and a traveler visited the Tokat Castle in 1656, and wrote down his experiences in the book titled, *Seyahatname*, meaning *My travels*. In the book, the mysterious castle with its secret tunnels and dungeons, where the brothers stayed at was described as follows:

"The dark castle was built with cut stone on a high hill. It was decorated with bastions and towers, and there was no moat around it. The walls of the castle protruded into the high-sky. When looking out from any one of the towers, it was steep on all corners. The castle was surrounded by falcon and eagle nests, and various colorful rocks. It has a west facing front wide entrance door. Inside the castle, there are multiple rooms, including, imam, muezzin, and prayer rooms. Plus, ammunition, grain warehouses, water cisterns, and a narrow tunnel gloomy walkway that leads down to the cold waters of the river. The wide entrance door was closed day and night, and no person could freely get out. The guards were always waiting and standing ready with guns and rifles. All the criminals, murderers, and hostages of Tokat, and surrounding area are imprisoned here, in the dungeons below the castle."

Tokat Castle

At the capital city of Edirne, the brothers joined other princes and elite individual's children to receive proper education. At Edirne, the brothers, Vlad 13 and Radu being six years old, received education, including, military tactics, Ottoman Turkish, and reading of the Quran. Furthermore, the brothers received intense religion lessons from *Molla Gurani*, who was a well-respected religious scholar, professor, and imam in the empire; his full name was *Semsuddin Ahmed bin Ismail bin Osman Gurani*.

Among the princes the brothers were educated alongside with were *Skanderbeg*, who would be the future Albanian feudal lord and military commander. And Prince Mehmet, the future ruler of the Ottoman Empire, known as Conqueror Sultan Mehmet. The brothers and Prince Mehmet became close friends and swore an oath of brotherhood between themselves. The brothers and Prince Mehmet went through the same education, and it should be noted here that Mehmet was only one year younger than Vlad. Their friendship grew so strong that they swore they would support each other until death.

It is believed that both brothers converted to the religion of Islam, and became successful recruits for the Ottoman

Empire. The plan was to eventually send both Vlad and Radu back to their native lands, and to rule in accordance, and in partnership with the empire.

The brothers were treated well by the standards of the period. Nonetheless, the separate lives of the brothers developed and progressed into a rather intriguing story for each one.

Radu would become an Ottoman governor in the Balkans region, and fully supported the empire. On the other hand, Vlad would become a fierce Ottoman enemy, and spent his entire adult life fighting both his younger brother and the empire.

Vlad was bitter at being captive, and always kept a hidden hostility toward the empire; this would be the main factor that motivated him to fight against them in the future. He wanted to avenge the days the empire held him in captivity.

While Vlad and Radu were living inside the territories of the Ottoman Empire, their father, Vlad Dracul was trying to maintain his position as the ruler of Wallachia. Unfortunately, his position as the ruler would end, and in 1447, Vlad was deposed by the native nobility, and murdered at the outskirts of *Targoviste*, the capital city.

In the same year in Wallachia, with Vladislav as the new ruler, another bloody war was fought to gain independence from the Hungarian Empire. Wallachia won the war, and declared independence; it was now an independent country.

The following year in 1448, when Vlad was 19 years old, he led a war campaign at the head of the Ottoman janissaries against Wallachia. Vlad wanted to avenge the death of his father, by killing Vladislav, who was one of the culprits that assassinated his father. The plan by the Ottoman Empire was to recapture

Wallachia, and Vlad would be placed on the throne. However, the campaign was not successful for Vlad and the empire. Therefore, he sought refuge back in the Ottoman Empire, before the end of the year.

The following year in 1449, Vlad went to *Hungary*, here he presented himself as the son of Vlad Dracul, the previous ruler of Wallachia. In Hungary, Vlad was received with respect and admiration, and a partnership quickly blossomed with the Hungarian Empire. Right about this time, Vlad changed his side, meaning, he became an ally to Hungary. He provided military support against the pockets of Ottoman governors north of the *Danube River*.

The news of the fall of Constantinople in 1453 to the Ottoman Empire was not well received in Hungary, and the rest of Europe. After the fall of the grand city, the

Ottomans were in a position to invade all of the European continent. Vlad's political and military side completely came to the forefront, as he was wanting and wishing to be a major actor in stopping the advancement by the eastern empire.

Vlad could not wait on the sidelines too long, living in Hungary, as he had big ambitions, the main determination being, to be the next ruler of Wallachia. Therefore, in 1456, with the help of the Hungarian Empire, he invaded Wallachia, and invited Vladislav, who was his uncle, and the ruler of Wallachia for a sword fight. The winner would be the ruler of Wallachia.

On July 22, 1456, Vlad and Vladislav agreed to settle the dispute in a single sword fight, in front of their armies. Vlad won by striking a killing blow to the chest of Vladislav.

Vlad regained his father's ruling seat, plus, he was successful in avenging his father's death, at the hands of the native nobility, particularly, Vladislav. Thus, Vlad's reign began at the young age of 28, in his birth home of Wallachia.

Welcome to my house. Come freely. Go safely; and leave something of the happiness you bring. --- Bram Stoker

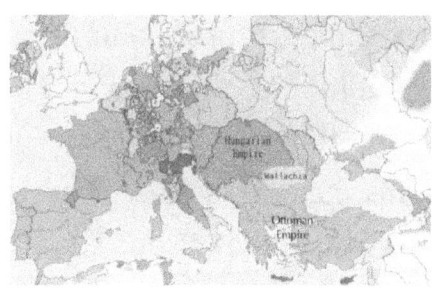

Map of the year 1500

The ruler, Vlad started by trying to strengthen his position with the elite noblemen of Wallachia; he did this by granting favors to them. However, he came into conflict with certain noblemen, who supported his opponents, *Dan* and *Basarab Laiota*, who were Vladislav's cousins. The first few months of his rule saw increased crime, corruption, and hunger in Wallachia.

Due to the increased crime in Wallachia, particularly in *Targoviste*, Vlad adopted the method of punishment that made him be called, *the Impaler*. Apart from impaling people, he became famous for various other gruesome tortures committed on his citizens. Additionally, the blood, flesh, and corpses of the victims were used to frighten his many enemies. These strange and abnormal tactics used, soon created rumors and tales about him being a vampire.

Vlad continuously plundered neighboring villages and towns to keep funds and resources coming into his kingdom. The people who revolted against him, met with his extreme cruelty. He would burn innocent people alive, without distinguishing between women, children, and older individuals; everyone was at his mercy. Vlad's wrath spread throughout the Balkans, everyone heard about his actions, and were fearful.

After settling in nicely as the new ruler of Wallachia, and starting to feel comfortable and powerful in his position, he ordered the stopping of the annual tribute given to the Ottoman Empire. This tribute or tax was sent to the empire to ensure peace in Wallachia. As a previously well-trained janissary soldier in the Ottoman Empire, Vlad the Impaler knew what conflict he was heading into, and he welcomed it wholeheartedly.

Finally, a few months after being the ruler, a letter arrived from his brother and current ruler of the Ottoman Empire,

Conqueror Sultan Mehmet. The letter read, "Vlad my brother from the olden days, since you are the ruler of Wallachia, and since this precious land is in my vast domain, you need to start paying your taxes." Paying taxes was going to acknowledge that Vlad was a puppet ruler, inside the Ottoman lands, therefore he could not allow this.

Saddened by the news he heard about the tortures committed onto the people in the Balkans region of Europe, plus, the unpaid tax, Sultan Mehmet decided to end Vlad's rule. The sultan wanted to instead place Radu, Vlad's brother as the new ruler in Wallachia. For this reason, he sent a message to Vlad asking him to come personally for a visit to the capital city of *Istanbul* of the Ottoman Empire.

Vlad the Impaler knew how his childhood friend and brothers mind worked; he understood the purpose of the sultan's insistence for a visit. If he went, the sultan would jail him. Vlad sent a message to the sultan that he would come for the visit, but an Ottoman governor should meet him at the banks of the *Danube River*, together they could ride to the capital city together. Sultan Mehmet agreed, and assigned *Hamza Bey*, an Ottoman Pasha to the task.

While Hamza Bey and his men were waiting for Vlad to arrive at the chosen location, one late evening, they faced an unexpected attack by the Wallachian ruler. Hamza Bey and his men were captured by Vlad's army, and brutally impaled. Conqueror Sultan Mehmet was shocked at receiving the news and learning that Hamza Bey and his men were violently impaled. He ordered all Balkan governors to make preparations for war.

As if playing with fire was not enough, meaning, starting a confrontation with the mighty Ottoman Empire by killing Hamza Bey and his men, Vlad's band of soldiers infiltrated the camp of the empire, disguised as Ottoman janissaries. Vlad's men killed over 20,000 Ottoman janissaries in a short period of time, in the Balkans region of the empire.

Furthermore, wanting to strengthen his power as the ruler, Vlad wanted to suppress the incessant conflicts with a few Wallachian elite noblemen, who supported one of the family members of the previous ruler of Vladislav. One evening, Vlad invited these noblemen to a feast, here, he gave the command to kill them all. Afterward, he ordered the bodies to be placed on stakes, at the outskirts of Targoviste; everyone needed to see, how he treated individuals that were against him.

Vlad's victories over the Ottomans, plus actions against his enemies and ruthless individuals in Targoviste were celebrated in Wallachia, Hungary, and throughout the rest of Europe. *Pope Pius II* heard of the actions by Vlad, he was witnessed to have made the following comment, "He is a popular character in Wallachia, because he is an exceedingly fair ruler for all his severe cruelty."

Upon hearing further stories about Vlad's cruelty, and attacks on the Ottoman camps in the Balkans, Conqueror Sultan Mehmet immediately sent 50,000 janissaries to bring down Vlad, plus take Wallachia. This war resulted in a stalemate between the Ottomans and Vlad's army, yet, 15,000 janissaries were killed.

When Sultan Mehmet heard the unproportionate number of deaths in his army, he was furious; he could not wait in *Istanbul* any longer. The sultan, with his 80,000 janissaries started the journey to Targoviste, the capital of Wallachia.

On the outskirts of the capital, the sultan and his army saw thousands of bodies, including women and children impaled. Sultan Mehmet and his army were shocked and surprised at his once brothers wicked actions against, not only his own people, but visiting messengers, and Ottoman janissaries.

The area where the bodies were impaled was three kilometers long by one kilometer wide. Long stakes were erected on the ground, and about 20,000 bodies were brutally impaled. At seeing such an unbelievable gruesome scene, the morale of the Ottoman janissaries deteriorated rapidly, while a few lost their minds. Sultan Mehmet realized right then and there that Vlad was not the same person that he sat alongside, and received his education with. This person, this wicked ruler of Wallachia was an insane and crazy man.

During the brief war against the Ottoman Empire, which went down in the history books as the night raid at Targoviste, Vlad's army almost killed Sultan Mehmet. It is believed that during the night raid, Vlad's men entered the wrong tent; not the sultan's tent. Although this was a real blow to the empire, Vlad's army had to flee because they could not withstand the brutal combat of the Ottomans, under Sultan Mehmet's command.

While Vlad escaped, he poisoned all the wells and springs, burned crops, and released imprisoned criminals, who had contagious disease onto the Ottoman camp. This type of warfare was never before witnessed by the Ottomans, and much suffering occurred by the janissaries. Nonetheless, even with the raid and disease onslaught by Vlad's army, it was a crushing victory on June 4, 1462, for the Ottoman Empire.

Vlad the Impaler hid in *Poenari Castle*, which is a structure built on the summit of a steep mountain at an altitude of 900 meters. It is a castle that resembles an eagle's nest that is almost inaccessible. It was rumored that the Sultan Mehmet, who surrounded the castle with his janissaries, sent a final message, "Vlad you are surrounded, give yourself over, or prepare for your last battle."

Poenari Castle

The Ottomans made preparations to surround the castle, but unfortunately for the empire, the siege continued for over a month. Vlad knew the empires strategy well, therefore, made a good defense. However, it was evident that the castle would be conquered soon enough.

Prior to conquering the Poenari Castle and capturing Vlad, the ruler of Wallachia escaped through the underground secret tunnels, and retreated deep into Hungary. Conqueror Sultan Mehmet placed Radu the Fair, Vlad's brother, at the throne of Wallachia, and made his way back to the capital city of Istanbul.

In Hungary, Vlad requested assistance from *Matthias Corvinus, King of Hungary*, in the latter part of the year 1462. Hungary had recognized and accepted Radu as the new ruler of Wallachia; a ruler that was loyal to the Ottoman Empire. Plus, they did not want to provoke the eastern empire into a war, therefore, they did not accept the request for help from Vlad. Instead, King Corvinus had Vlad imprisoned in the city of *Visegrad* from the years, 1462 to 1475.

In 1476, with the support of the Moldovan ruler, *Stephen the Great*, Vlad was released from prison, and made another effort to regain the ruling seat of Wallachia. He successfully took the throne, but his victory was short-lived.

Here, the mystery of Vlad began. He had come back from prison, or another way of stating, he came back from the dead to take the throne. Vlad, who was imprisoned for 13 long years was released, and he returned to Wallachia. The citizens of Wallachia were astounded, and echoed the cry of, "He has risen again from the earth."

Vlad the Impaler, who was thought to be dead, came back to these lands, and became not only a symbol of fear and terror for many, but an idol to some individuals.

No one is immortal in the mortal world. People's breaths on earth are numbered, and the gate of immortality is closed. --- Conqueror Sultan Mehmet II

Bust of Vlad Dracula located in present day, Bucharest, Romania

Why was Vlad's capturing of the throne in Wallachia short-lived? In 1476, Vlad and his army were ambushed by *Mihaloglu Ali*

Bey, an Ottoman Pasha, and his band of men. Vlad was killed instantaneously, and revenge was finally taken by the Ottoman Empire. Vlad's head was put in a barrel full of honey, so it did not spoil rapidly. Afterward, it was sent to Istanbul, for Conqueror Sultan Mehmet to view, and confirm that the severed head belonged to Vlad, and he was dead.

Vlad's head was put on a long stake, just like he did to his victims in Wallachia. Furthermore, his head was wandered around the streets of Istanbul, as an example for everyone to see what happens to an enemy of the empire.

There are different theories about the whereabouts of Vlad's headless grave. In keeping with the tradition of his time, meaning, when a ruler died, the preferred burial location was at *Snagov Monastery*, just on the outskirts of Targoviste. The monastery was the preferred burial location of noble persons of Wallachia, during these times.

Snagov Monastery

However, there are other theories that Vlad was actually buried at *Comana Monastery*, just south of the present-day city of *Bucharest*. The reason this monastery might also be the believed location of Vlad's grave is that, this was close to where he was killed by the Ottoman Pasha.

Romania encompasses the territories where Vlad the Impaler or Vlad Dracula was born and ruled in. Therefore, this country, and parts of the surrounding area of Europe continues to see Vlad as a hero, even though he was a cruel and brutal ruler. There are two reasons for this, one reason was, Vlad's army was the last Christian stronghold to stop the Ottoman janissary's further advancement into Europe. The second reason was due to the influence Vlad had on the legendary novel titled, Dracula by Bram Stroker.

Poenari Castle, which was the home of Vlad is now a museum in Romania. The castle is currently surrounded by multiple souvenir shops with Vlad's scary pictures on their walls. The entire area has become a tourist attraction.

History is full of unforgettable and notable characters. Among these characters, there are those whose names are remembered for their objective administration, humanitarian philosophies, and courageous battles.

Additionally, there are those who are mentioned by their cruelty, brutality, and fear they caused and spread. One of the characters from recent history that dispensed the most cruelty was certainly, Vlad Dracula, who lived in the 15th century. However, he achieved real fame and notoriety at the beginning of the 19th century, due to the book by Bram Stoker, titled Dracula.

Have you read the legendary novel?

Who was Vlad The Impaler?

Let's start from the begin… Vlad III Dracula, Prince of Wallachia, was

born in 1431, in Sighisoara, a city in Transylvania. He is the son of Vlad II and nephew of Mircea cel Batran (the Elder), being part of the Bessarabian dynasty. His father, Vlad II, was a knight in the Order of the Dragon, a knightly order from Eastern Europe, founded in 1408 by Sigismund of Luxembourg, that aimed to stop the expansion of the Ottoman Empire. The symbol of the Order was a dragon, and its purpose was to defend Christianity and crusade the Ottoman counterattacks. And Vlad II was so proud that he and crusade the Ottoman counterattacks. And Vlad II was so proud that he 1442; 1443-1447), he had that dragon fought and carved, as an emblem of him from where among the people, his name was Vlad Dracul (after "draco" in Latin, which means "dragon"). This name will be passed on to his son, with an "a" added at the end, which suggests the possessive case of the noun. Thus, "Dracula" actually means "of the Dracul" / "of the Dragon". Cliché, in Romanian "Dracul" means "the Devil", so it was easy for many who did not know the origin of his name to interpret other things at that time.

Against the background of the Ottoman suzerainty over Wallachia, Vlad II is suspected of infidelity by the Sultan and the Ottoman Gate, and in the spring of 1442, he is imprisoned and forced to leave his children - Vlad Dracula and his brother, Radu - in the hands of the Ottoman Empire.

Vlad III was a hostage until 1448, and his brother until 1462. This life of captivity played an important role in the formation and rise of Vlad's power. The Turks released him, in 1447, after the death of his father - assassinated at the command of Vladislav II (other one, excluded from Draculesti line), rival to the throne of Wallachia. At the same time, Vlad found out about the death of his older brother, Mircea, tortured and buried alive by the boyars from Târgoviște.

At the age of 17, supported by a Turkish cavalry corps and a contingent of troops lent to him by Mustafa Hassan, Vlad Drăculea took over the reign of Wallachia for the first time. But, two months later, he was defeated by Vladislav II, who regained his throne. To secure his second and longest reign, Vlad III had to wait until August 20, 1456, when he managed to kill his mortal enemy.

The first important act of revenge was directed against the boyars from Târgoviște, guilty of the death of their father and brother. On Easter Sunday, 1459, he arrested all the boyar families who had attended the princely feast. The oldest were impaled, and the others were forced to walk a hundred kilometers from the capital to Poenari, where they were forced to build a fortress on the ruins of an old outpost overlooking the Argeş River. But the favorite torture was the impaling, from which comes the nicknameȚepeş, the one who impaled.

The conflict with the Ottoman Empire
In 1459, Vlad the Impaler refused to pay tribute to the Turks (10,000

coins a year). It seems that this revolt was due to the existence of a crusade project against the Ottomans, a crusade supported by the Pope and in which the King of Hungary, Matthias Corvinus, was to play the leading role. team 12,000 men and 10 warships). In this political context, VladȚepeş concluded an alliance with Matei Corvin, probably at the beginning of 1460, which the Ottomans would have wanted to prevent. Moreover, they will try, through Hamza Pasha, the drunkard of Nicopolis, and the deacon of the sultan, Catavolinos, to catch Vlad by trickery, but without success. Once the plans of the Ottomans were thwarted and punished (the two were impaled along with all the Turkish soldiers who accompanied them), Vlad the Impaler organized a surprise campaign south of the Danube in the winter of 1461-1462.A large region, from Obluciţa to Novoe Selo and from the Danube to the Black Sea to Rahova, was devastated. Moreover, the fortress of Nicopolis being slyly occupied, over 20,000 Turks perished under the weapons of the Wallachians, the number of those killed being indicated by VladŢepeş himself in a letter addressed to Matei Corvin. Also in this letter, sent from Giurgiu on February 11, 1462, Vlad insisted on the Hungarian king's support. Although he assured him on March 4, 1462, that he would come to his aid, Matthew Corvinus left Buda only at the end of August, when the Ottoman campaign was already over.

As for Muhammad II, he, surprised by Țepeș's defiance, will prepare a suitable 's defiance, will prepare a suitable 120,000 men (the second largest after that to conquer Constantinople) plus 175

warships whose purpose was to conquer Chilia, will head for Danube. The Wallachian army did not exceed 30,000 troops, according to the most generous estimates. Although Vlad tries to stop the Turks on the Danube, near the Turnu fortress, they, under the shelter of the night, manage to cross the river heading directly towards Târgoviște (June 4, 1462). Under these conditions, Țepeș will apply the tactic of harassment: desolation of the land - especially the road to Târgoviște -, poisoning of wells, attack of Turkish detachments gone for food. In this oppressive atmosphere in which the Turkish armies, hungry and frightened, were advancing through the deserted country, took place the great blow of Vlad the Impaler, the night attack of June 16-17, 1462, meant to further demoralize the Ottoman army. The Wallachians surrounded the Turks and destroyed them with gunfire. Historians believe Vlad to be one of the first European crusaders to use gunpowder "in a creative deadly way". In a letter to King Matei Corvin, dated February 2, 1462, he wrote that Hamza Pasha had been captured near the former Wallachian fortress of Giurgiu. After destroying Hamza Pasha, Vlad disguised himself in Turkish clothes and advanced with his cavalry to the fortress, where he ordered the Turkish guards to open the gates. They complied, and Vlad attacked and destroyed the Turkish forces in the fortress. The target of the attack was the sultan himself, but he escaped, his tent being confused with that of a vizier. However, the psychological effect of the attack was significant. Many Turks were killed and the sultan reportedly "secretly left the camp in disgrace"; seeing the "great loss suffered by his own" he ordered a withdrawal. Near Târgoviște, a spectacle awaited him that terrified his armies: a forest of thorns in which hung a multitude of Turks killed before or during the battle; In the face of this, the Turks "were very frightened," and the sultan acknowledged that "he cannot take the land of a man who does such great things" and who "would be worthy of more." After that, a campaign began to destroy the Turks and the people who helped them; first in southern Wallachia, then in Bulgaria,

crossing the frozen Danube. In Bulgaria, he divided his army into several small groups and covered about 800 kilometers in two weeks, destroying more than 23,000 Turks and Bulgarians.

In a letter to Corvin, dated February 11, 1462, Vlad wrote:

"We killed men and women, old and young, residents of Obluci a and Novoselo, wherethe Danubeflowsinto thesea,to Rahova, which is nearChilia, below theDanubeto places like Samovitand Ghighen. Wekilled 23,884 Turks and Bulgarians not counting thoseweburned

intheirhomes   orthosewhoseheads
werenot   cut   offby   oursoldiers
....SoYourHighness   must   know
thatwehavebrokenthepeacewith
he[sultan]".

With the exception of the Turkish chronicles, all other sources testify to the defeat of the sultan, who was forced "to flee back to the Danube with great losses among his people and the shame of having turned his back." The Turkish army headed for the Danube, so quickly that on July 11, 1462, the sultan had reached Adrianople. According to the Byzantine chronicler Chalcocondil, the sultan leftȚepeș's brother, Radu cel Frumos (the Handsome), to Târgoviște on his way, in order for him to attract to his side all those who opposedȚepeș.

Radu cel Frumos

Radu is Vlad Tepes' younger

brother. Against the background of the accusations brought against their father for deception and betrayal, Vlad and

Radu, in 1442, as children, are brought and forced to remain in the Ottoman Empire, being raised and educated according to Islamic law. Some rumors claim that the two were tortured and even molested, which led to Vlad Tepes' irremediable hatred for the Ottomans and to the preferred method of punishment, the impaling, as revenge against the Turks for the traumas suffered or as an element that remained subconsciously in his memory, while his brother remained controlled by these customs and aroused a deep attachment to the sultan. It is also said that Radu's attachment to the sultan had a different connotation, his favoritism and loyalty to the sultan being based on intimate acts between the two, which led to the nickname "the Handsome", which actually suggests that he would have been gay. At the same time, Nicolae Iorga - Romanian historian and academician, among others - in

Lett ersofboyars, lettersofgentlemen, supposes the same thing. Specifically, the historian suspects that Vlad and Radu were abused. Vlad came to hate the Ottomans and wanted to punish them, while Radu became a follower of the practices, becoming a lover of the Sultan. "Vlad gave both his sons, one after the other, to the Turks: Vlad (The Impaler), who learns cruelty there, and Radu (the Handsome), who chose to be depraved", Iorga shows in the mentioned work. In fact, the Greek chronicler Laonic Chalkocondyl describes the first attempt directed against Radu:"And the boy, without suspecting that such a thing would happen to the Emperor, saw the Emperor rushing to him for such a thing, and he resisted, and did not yield to the Emperor's wish. He kissed him against his will and the boy, taking out a dagger, struck the Emperor in the thigh and so he ran away, wherever he could. The doctors healed the Emperor's wound ", says the chronicler, after a translation by Vasile Grecu. After hiding, Radu realized that he would not escape anyway and voluntarily went to the sultan, eventually becoming his partner. "But after the King had packed his bags and left, the boy also got down from the tree and took her on his way, not long afterwards he came to the Gate and became the Emperor's favorite." At the same time, he states that Radu's brother, Vlad (Ţepeş), was also called to the Gate. "This winter, however, the Emperor, spending it in his palaces, sent for Vlad, the son of Draculea, lord of Dacia." Vlad would have been subjected to similar treatment. That is why VladŢepeş would have hated the Turks in particular, subjecting them to horrible riots. His greatest desire was to kill the Sultan. However, there are many Romanian and foreign historians who say that there is not enough data to support this hypothesis and that it cannot be said with certainty that Vlad was abused in the Ottoman Empire. Moreover, Radu cel Frumos is often illustrated with feminine features.

RaducelFrumosbyElveo onDeviantArt
Vlad epe, PrinceofWallachia

Dracula's Castle

Bran Castle is a historical monument

located 25 kilometers from Brasov and is the symbol of Transylvania. Bran Castle is often confused with
Dracula's Castle in Bram Stocker's novel "Dracula".

Dracula, the main character of the book of the same name written at the end of the 19th century, is a Transylvanian count, owner of a castle built on top of a high cliff, from where it rises the river valley meandering through the Transylvanian Principality.

Bram Stocker has never visited Romania. In the description of Dracula's fictional Castle, he starts from a presentation of Bran Castle available in England at that time. Indeed, the castle, as it appears in the printed engraving from the first edition of the novel Dracula, bears a striking resemblance to Bran Castle and only to it.

Even so, in reality, Vlad Dracula did not have so many connections with this castle. His main residence is at the Royal Citadel of Targoviste, Sighisoara, and his second at the Poenari Forteress.

Poenari   Fortress
TheRoyalCitadyofTargoviste

Vlad The Impaler and his ladies

Anastasia   Holszanska
Vlad Tepes' first wife was Anastasia Holszanska, the niece of the Queen of

Poland. Not much is known about their story. The date of her birth is not known, but it is known that she died in 1462, at the Poenari Fortress, by suicide, throwing herself from the top of the tower into the turbulent waters of the river Arges. For this reason, the Arges River is also called the Lady River. The exact cause of her suicide is unknown. Some sources report that she thrown herself from the city walls on the night of an Ottoman attack, after receiving a letter stating that Vlad had been defeated in battle. Fearing that she would be taken hostage by her enemies, she preferred to end her days. Other sources suggest that Anastasia committed suicide out of jealousy when she found out about her husband's mistress, a young Saxon woman named Katharina Siegel from Brasov.

Katharina Siegel

The 18th-century Transylvanian chronicle reveals

rare details from Ţepeş's life, during his stay in Braşov, between 1451 and 1456. Among other unique information about him, there is also one that refers to a beautiful young woman of Saxon origin that Vlad Țepeș loved very much. The well-known Romanian ruler was a rather charismatic man, so apart from the

three well-known marriages, he had many other love affairs which resulted in illegitimate children. Before becoming the ruler of Wallachia, in the winter of 1455, ValdȚepeș met the woman who would become his great love, the Saxon Katharina Siegel, who was then only 17 years old.

The story of the two begins in December 1455. The young Katharina, then 17 years old, was struggling to pull through the snow a sledge loaded with snacks for the soldiers of the Weavers' Bastion, located on a hill in Corona. When the voivode saw the young girl struggling, he jumped to her aid, to the surprise of the officers who accompanied him and who knew that Ţepeş had never made such a generous gesture to anyone. In love with the young Saxon woman, Ţepeş resorted to all sorts of strategies to seduce her, one of the gestures being to order her the most beautiful silk dresses and chosen lace, from Venice and Flanders.

Katharina suffered from the horrors of Dracula. According to the chronicles, on April 2, 1459, angry with the high taxes imposed by the Saxons from Braşov and the intrigues of the city chiefs, vladţepeş destroyed all the grain crops in Ţara Bârsei. He ordered the capture of hundreds of merchants and merchants who came with goods to the fortress, which he took to the slum of the city, in the area of today's Bartholomew, and stabbed them. In the morning, the bloody ruler ate breakfast among the dying agonists dragged to the stake. After their death, he ordered the robbery and burning of Bartolomeu Church, as well as the burning of Codlea village.

Because the love story between Katharina and Stepeş was known in the fair,

the merchants' wives wanted to take revenge on the voivode's mistress and attacked the house where she lived. They beat her and put her on the Pillar of Infamy. Because her hair tails were cut off, the ruler threatened to set fire to the entire city. As Katharina was being held captive,Ţepeş had to escape his girlfriend, so he had to release the other Saxon merchants who were to be killed.

Țepeș asked the Sovereign Pontiff to annul his first marriage so that he could marry Katharina. Vlad Tepes wanted to marry Katharina, but the rigors of religion did not allow him, although he had several children with his mistress from Brasov. He even wrote twice to the Sovereign Pontiff, Pope Pius II, asking for a letter of indulgence to annul his marriage to his first wife, Anastasia Holszanska.

During the love affair between the two, Katharina gave birth to a number of three babies: Vladislav (1456), Catherina (1459) and Christian (1461). After completing the episode in which Anastasia committed suicide, throwing herself off the walls of the Poenari Fortress, Vlad was finally free and able to marry Katharina, but a plot by his former rivals ends with Țepeș's imprisonment at Buda, where Matei Corvin takes He said he would release him on the condition that he marry his aunt, Elizabeth Corvinus of Hunyadi.

Thus, Țepeș failed to formalize his relationship with Katharina. But she had two more children with her - Hanna and Sigismund. Although he was married, Katharina remained close to "Dracula" even after his fall from the throne in 1462, andȚepeș took care of all his descendants, as evidenced by the 1850 land books of the Draguly, Laszlo or Siegel families.

The assassination of the voivode, in 1477, put an end to the love between him and Katharina, and the beautiful woman who conquered "Dracula" to her death returned to the monastery.

Justina   Szilagyi
Betrayed by the boyars who had staged a letter to his counterpart - the king of Hungary, Matthias Corvinus -, Vlad Tepes was captured in 1462 and held hostage by the king, which prevented his

plan to formalize his marriage to Katharina Siegel. Vlad was released in 1476 on the condition imposed by Matthias Corvinus that he marry his cousin, Justina Szilagyi. Thus, Justina Szilagyi (or Ilona, according to some sources), the cousin of the Hungarian despot, Matthias Corvinus and the niece of Queen Elisabeta Szilagyi's mother, becomes the second wife of the Voivode, Lady of the Romanian Country.

The Death

In 1462, Vlad the Impaler ended his second reign. Although victorious in a battle against the Turks, he is forced to go to Transylvania in search of allies. The Ottomans left Radu cel Frumos as lord in Târgoviște, assisted by Pasha of Nicopolis. At the same time, the boyars sided with the pretender chosen by the Turks, who was VladȚepeș's good brother, moments with ranks, but also with thoughts of peace. On the other hand, Țepeș hoped to obtain support from the king of Hungary, Matei Corvin, in order to regain his throne. The enemies of the voivode of Muntenia, however, wrote a compromising letter. More precisely, through this letter,Țepeș's opponents wanted to create the impression that the voivode of Muntenia would like to close himself to the Turks and go with them in a campaign against Transylvania.

The letter ended up in the hands of the king of Hungary, and the fate ofȚepeș was decided. Not only did he not offer armed aid to the voivode of Muntenia, but he also set a trap for him. More precisely, Matei Corvin ordered the arrest of VladȚepeș. The voivode of Muntenia was taken and imprisoned for 12 years in the fortress of Visegrad. In 1474, Vlad the Impaler was released and remained in the service of the King of Hungary. For a year, he fought on behalf of the Hungarian crown in the Balkans, and in 1476, only after a failed attempt, he was again supported to take the throne of Wallachia. This time the one who supported Țepeș was the voivode of Moldova, Ștefan cel Mare (Stephen the Great). He was launching a new antiOttoman and antimunitions campaign. And this in the conditions in which his protégé Laiota Basarab, placed by Stephen